The clever crow

An Aesop's Fable

Retold by Beverley Randell Illustrated by Mini Goss

It was a very hot day.
A big black bird called a crow
wanted a drink of water.

3

The crow flew to a tree
and he looked down.
"Where is some water?"
he said.
"Where can I find a drink?"

Then he saw a pot.

The crow flew down
from the tree
to have a good look
at the pot.

Yes!
There was some water
inside it.

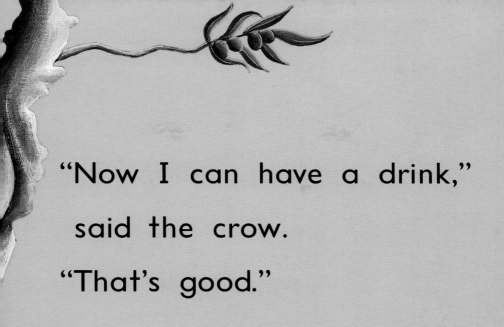

"Now I can have a drink,"
said the crow.
"That's good."

But the crow
was a big bird.
His head was too big
to get inside the pot.

"I do want a drink,"
he said.
"But I can't put my beak
in the water."

The crow had to walk away without a drink.

Then he saw some stones.

He stopped and looked
at the stones for a long time.
Then he said,
"I can see a way
to get a drink!"

The crow
was a very clever bird.

The crow walked back
to the pot
with a stone in his beak.

He put the stone
in the pot.

Plop!

This made the water
in the pot
come up a little way.

The crow
put some more stones
into the pot, one by one.

Plop!

Plop!

Plop!

The water came up
inside the pot,
little by little.

And then the clever crow
had a drink of water!